MUSICAL INSTRUMENTS OF THE WORLD

Woodwind and Brass

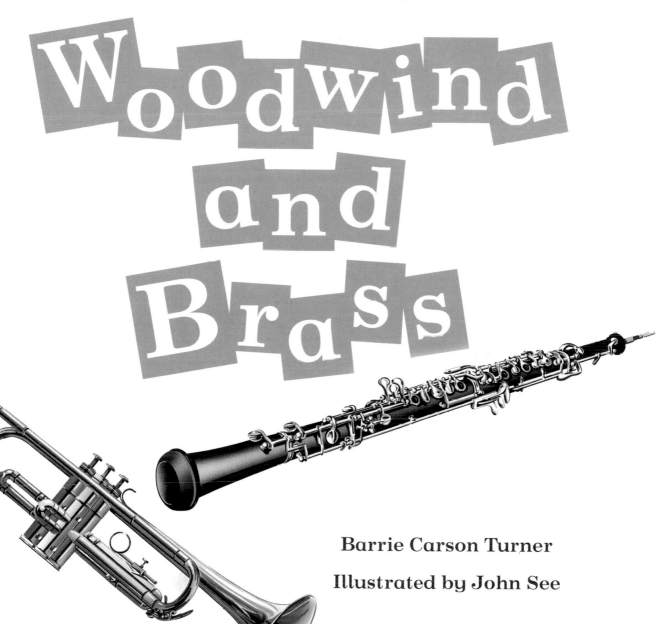

Barrie Carson Turner

Illustrated by John See

🌷 **Belitha Press**

First published in the UK in 1998 by
Belitha Press Limited
London House, Great Eastern Wharf,
Parkgate Road, London SW11 4NQ

Editor: Claire Edwards
Series designer: Simeen Karim
Picture researcher: Juliet Duff
Educational consultant: Celia Pardaens

ISBN 1 85561 791 9

Printed in Hong Kong / China

British Library Cataloguing in Publication Data
for this book is available from the British Library.

9 8 7 6 5 4 3 2 1

Picture acknowledgements Eye Ubiquitous: 10, 15 David Cumming;
Robert Harding Picture Library: 6 A. Woolfitt, 20-21 Rolf Richardson,
28-29 Ken Gilham; The Hutchison Library: 4-5 Trevor Page, 22 P. Moszynski;
Panos Pictures: 9; Performing Arts Library: 11-12 James McCormick,
16-17 Clive Barda; Redferns: 19, 26 Odile Noel, 23 Henrietta Butler,
24-25 David Redfern; Royal Scottish National Orchestra: 14 Stephen West;
Stock Market: 7, 27; Trip: 18 V. Sidoropolev; John Walmsley Photo Library: 8, 13.

Contents

Musical

Musical instruments are played in every country of the world. They are often grouped into four families: strings, brass, percussion and woodwind.

Brass and woodwind instruments are blown to make their sound. String instruments sound when their strings vibrate. Percussion instruments are struck (hit), shaken or scraped to make their sound.

instruments

For this book we have chosen 19 brass and woodwind instruments. Brass players press their lips tightly together and blow air through them to make their instruments sound. Woodwind instruments are made to sound in different ways. The ones in this book all have a reed which vibrates when the instrument is blown.

There is a picture of each instrument, and a photograph of a performer playing it. On pages 30 and 31 you will find a list of useful words to help you understand more about music.

B

W

On each page you will see a **B** or a **W** in a coloured box. **B** means the instrument is from the brass family. **W** means the instrument is from the woodwind family.

Oboe

The oboe is a long, thin instrument. A reed is fitted into the blowing end. This is made from two small pieces of cane tied together. Players hold the reed firmly in their mouth, and blow through it. Oboes make a beautiful sound. They often play solos in orchestras and ensembles.

reed

finger hole

key

Oboes have finger holes and keys. Oboe players (oboists) cover and uncover the holes, and press the keys to make different notes.

Trumpet

B

The trumpet is a well-known brass instrument. Its sound is exciting and loud. Trumpets are made from a long, tightly-coiled metal tube. One end has a mouthpiece. At the other end the tube opens out into a cone. This is called the bell.

bell

mouthpiece

valve

Players press down three small buttons, called valves, to make different notes. Trumpet players are called trumpeters. They play in orchestras and jazz bands.

7

Clarinet

mouthpiece

The clarinet has a wide range of notes, from low to very high. The player covers the finger holes and presses metal keys to make different notes. A thin flat piece of cane, called a reed, is fixed to the mouthpiece. When the clarinet player (clarinettist) blows into the mouthpiece, the reed vibrates and the instrument sounds.

finger hole

key

The clarinet can be heard in many different kinds of music, including orchestras, small ensembles and jazz groups.

Cornet

The cornet is made from a coiled metal tube. It is like a trumpet, but shorter, and its sound is not as bright. It has three buttons, called valves. When the player presses these, they open and close parts of the tube. This makes different notes.

valve

bell

mouthpiece

B

The cornet is usually played in brass bands. It often plays solo.

9

Conch

The conch is made from the shell of a large shellfish. The end of the shell is cut off or a hole is made in the side, and the instrument is blown like a trumpet. The conch has been used to call workers from the fields or to call soldiers to war. It is still played at religious festivals.

blow hole

The conch makes a loud sound which can carry long distances. It is sometimes called a shell trumpet. But unlike a trumpet, a conch can only sound one note.

B

Bassoon

crook

reed

The bassoon is a very large woodwind instrument. The finger holes are covered by small metal caps called keys. Near the top there is a curved metal tube called a crook. This makes it easier for players to reach the mouthpiece and the keys at the same time. Players wear a neck strap to help hold the instrument.

The bassoon sounds like an oboe, but its notes are much lower. Bassoon players (bassoonists) hold the reed tightly in their mouth and blow through it.

key

W

11

French horn

The French horn was brought to England from France 300 years ago, and has been called the French horn ever since. It is usually played in orchestras and brass bands. It is made from a long, coiled, shiny metal tube. Uncoiled, it would stretch several metres.

mouthpiece

B

bell

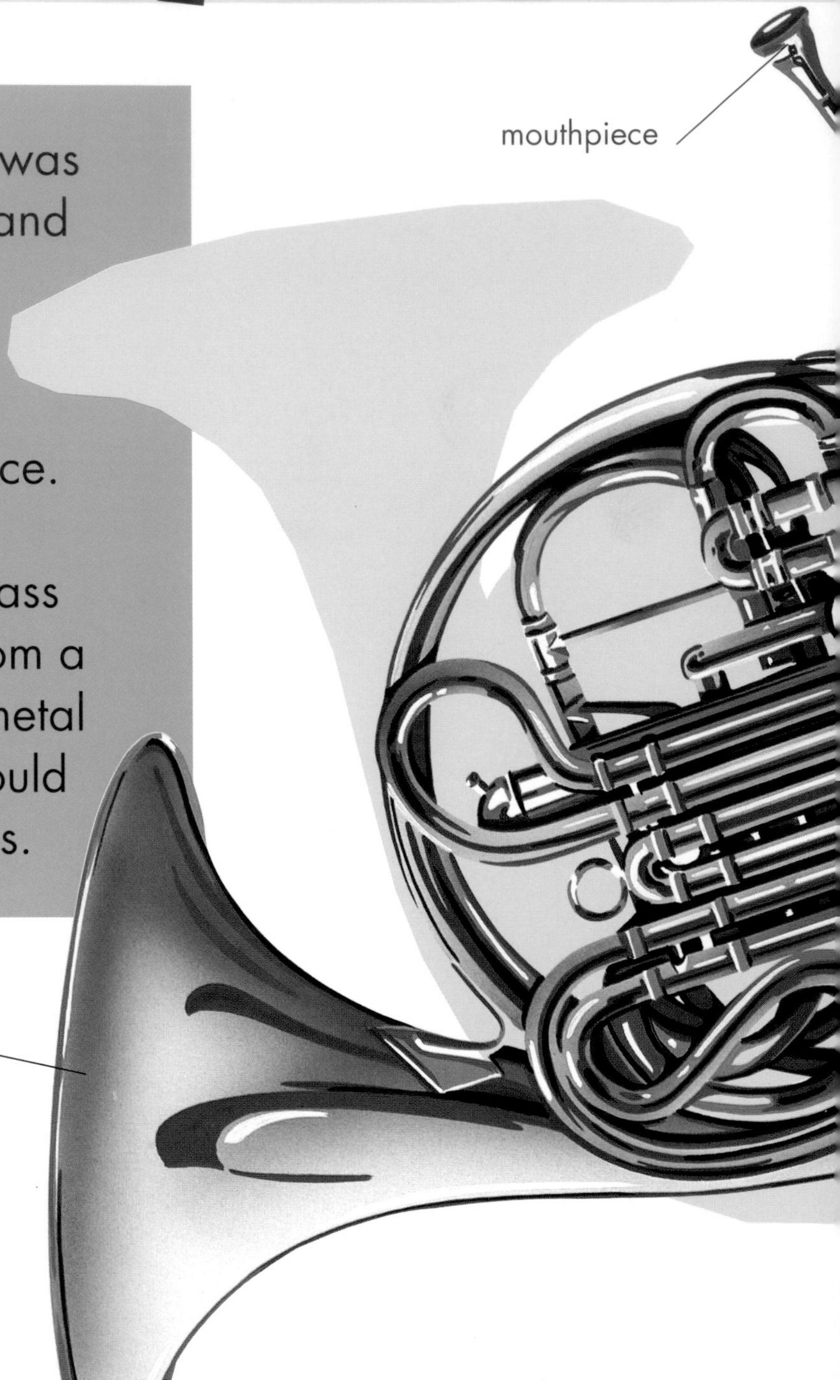

Players press down three small levers, called valves, to make many different notes. They push their lips tightly into the mouthpiece. By changing the shape of their lips they help to make the different notes. These can sound low and warm, or high and bright.

valve

French horn players place their right hand in the bell as they play. This helps to hold the horn and improve its sound.

Cor anglais

Cor anglais (cor-onglay) means English horn. It looks like a big oboe. Players blow through a reed, which is fitted into a long metal tube at the top. The bottom end is shaped like a pear, and is called the bell. Most of the finger holes are covered by small metal caps called keys.

reed

crook

W

key

bell

The cor anglais sounds lower than the oboe, but higher than a bassoon. It has a rich, dreamy sound.

14

Pungi

gourd

The pungi (pun-ji) comes from India. It has two pipes. One pipe sounds only one note. The player covers and uncovers finger holes on the other pipe to make different notes. The round body of the pungi is made from a gourd (a pear-shaped fruit).

W

finger hole

Players blow into one end of the gourd. They need a lot of breath to make the pungi's unusual whining sound.

Sousaphone

The sousaphone (sooz-a-fone) was named about 100 years ago after an American composer called John Philip Sousa. Sousa wanted a new brass instrument to play very low notes, so he decided to invent one.

B

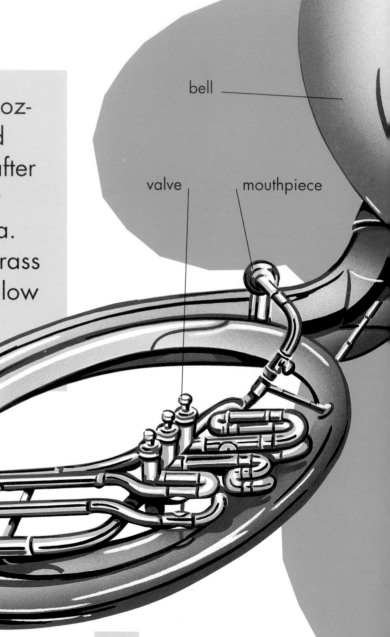

bell

valve

mouthpiece

Players press down small buttons, called valves, to make different notes. The valves open and close parts of the tube.

The sousaphone is so big, it has to be looped round the player's body and rests on the left shoulder. Its huge bell faces out towards the audience. Brass sousaphones are very heavy. Modern ones are often made from fibreglass, which is much lighter.

Zurna

reed

The zurna comes from Turkey. It is carved from wood, and is often decorated with silver. Like the oboe, it has two small pieces of cane fitted into the blowing end. They are shaped like a tiny fan and tied tightly together. This is called the reed.

The zurna is often played at weddings and festivals. The player holds the reed tightly in the mouth and blows through it to make a strong, buzzing sound.

finger hole

W

Trombone

The trombone is made from a long metal tube which is coiled round twice. At one end the tube opens out like a trumpet. Part of the tubing is called the slide. The player moves the slide in and out to make different notes. Trombone players are called trombonists. They must blow very hard when they play.

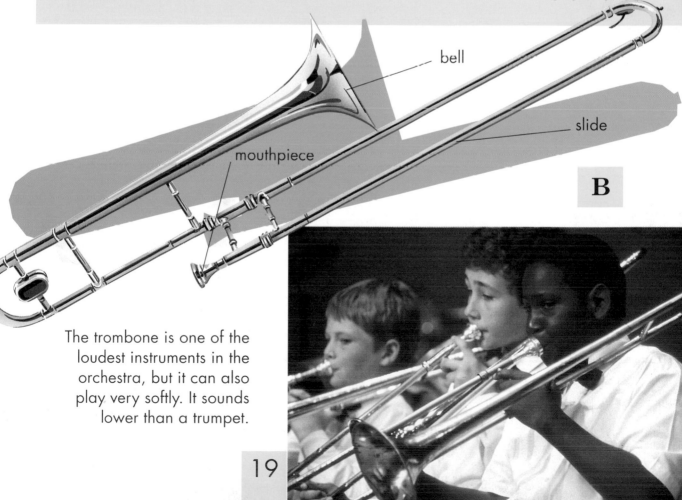

bell

slide

mouthpiece

B

The trombone is one of the loudest instruments in the orchestra, but it can also play very softly. It sounds lower than a trumpet.

Saxophone

The saxophone is made of metal, but it is a woodwind instrument. It was invented by a Belgian instrument maker called Adolphe Sax about 150 years ago. Like the clarinet, it has a flat piece of cane, called a reed, fixed to the mouthpiece with a thin band of metal. When the saxophone player blows into the mouthpiece, the reed vibrates, and the instrument sounds.

mouthpiece

The finger holes on a saxophone are covered by small metal keys. The player presses on the keys, which open and close the holes to make different notes.

W

key

bell

Saxophones are made in seven different sizes. The highest is called a sopranino. The lowest, called a contrabass, is about two metres long. Saxophones are usually played in jazz, rock and wind bands. They make a rich, smooth sound.

Sheng

pipe

The sheng is a mouth organ. It was first played in China thousands of years ago. At the bottom of each pipe there is a thin piece of metal called a reed. When air passes through the pipes, the reed vibrates and the instrument sounds. Each pipe plays a different note.

Players make the sheng sound by blowing and sucking through the mouthpiece.

W

finger hole

mouthpiece

Euphonium

The euphonium (u-fo-nium) is like a small tuba. It is made from a long metal tube coiled round many times. At the end, the tube widens into a large cone shape, called the bell. Players press down four small buttons, called valves, to make different notes.

B

bell

mouthpiece

valve

The euphonium is usually played in brass bands. You will often hear it playing a solo in a piece of music. Its sound is warm and mellow.

Accordion

The accordion is an unusual woodwind instrument. On one side it has a small piano keyboard. On the other side there are many finger buttons. In between there are bellows. Musicians play the tune on the keyboard. They press the buttons to play the accompaniment.

keyboard

W

The accordion often plays dance and folk music. It hangs around the player's neck by a strap. It makes a wheezy sound.

24

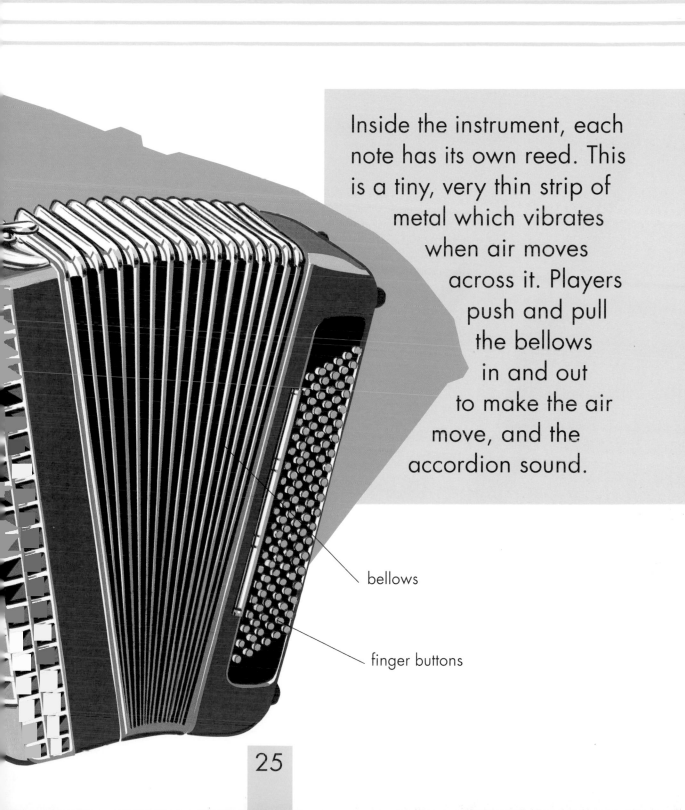

Inside the instrument, each note has its own reed. This is a tiny, very thin strip of metal which vibrates when air moves across it. Players push and pull the bellows in and out to make the air move, and the accordion sound.

bellows

finger buttons

Didjeridu

blowing
end

The didjeridu (di-jerri-doo) comes from Australia. It is made from a long, hollow tree branch. Players need a lot of breath to play the didjeridu. They press their lips tightly into the hollow tube, and blow through them to make a sound. It is important that no air escapes as they blow.

A didjeridu usually plays only one note, but players use their mouth, lips and voice to make the note sound in different ways.

hollow tube

B

Tuba

The tuba is the biggest and lowest-sounding brass instrument in an orchestra. Players press their lips tightly into the mouthpiece and blow to make a sound. They can help to make different notes by changing the shape of their lips as they blow. Because the tuba is so big, it takes a lot of breath to play.

bell

valve   mouthpiece

B

The tuba is played in orchestras and brass bands. Musicians play sitting down, with the tuba resting on their knees.

27

Bagpipes

Bagpipe players fill the instrument's bag with air by blowing into the blowpipe. The bag must be kept full of air all the time. Once it is full, the air can only escape through the pipes. Each pipe has a reed. When the bag is squeezed by the player's arm, the air is forced into the pipes, which makes them sound.

drone pipe

Bagpipes are played in many parts of the world. In Scotland they are played at important events. They have a shrill wailing sound, and can be heard over a long distance.

W

The larger pipes are called drones, and sound only one note. The tune is played on a smaller pipe called a chanter. Players cover and uncover the finger holes on the chanter pipe to make different notes.

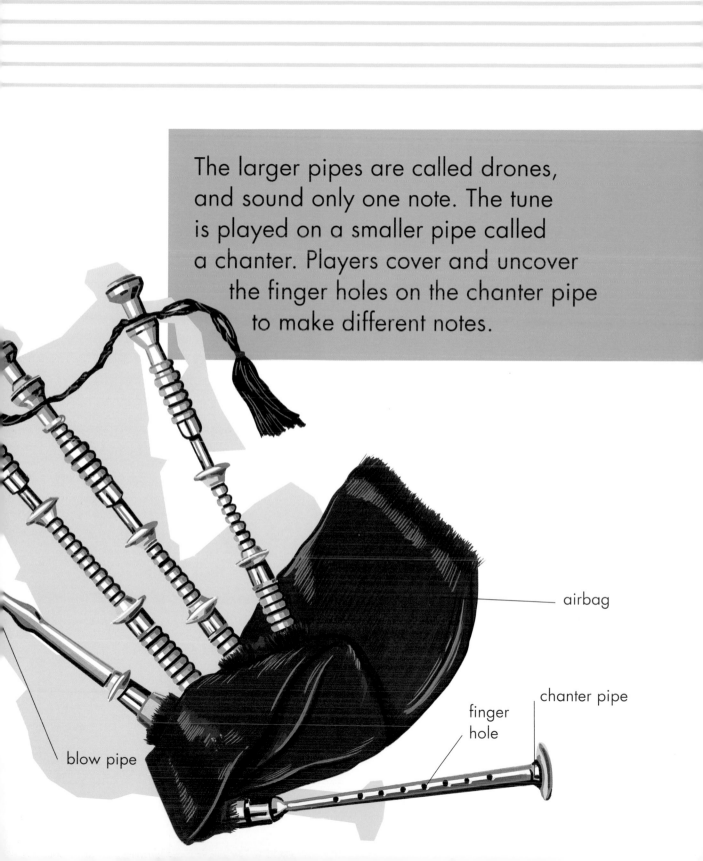

airbag

chanter pipe

finger hole

blow pipe

Words to

accompaniment Notes that are played along with the tune.

audience People who listen to musicians playing or singing.

bell The wide end of a brass or woodwind instrument.

bellows The part of an instrument that holds air. When a player squeezes the bellows, the instrument makes a sound.

brass band An orchestra of brass instruments.

composer A person who composes (writes) music.

crook An extra piece of tubing on some long instruments that helps players reach all the finger holes.

ensemble A small group of musicians playing together.

family (of instruments) Instruments that are similar to each other.

festival A special event, often with music and dancing.

fibreglass A material made of glass. It is lighter than metal.

finger holes The holes a player covers to make different notes.

folk music Popular songs or tunes that are so old, no one knows who wrote them.

jazz A kind of pop music. In jazz, musicians often make up the music at the same time as they play it.

keyboard Notes, called keys, laid out as they are on a piano.

key (on a woodwind instrument) A small metal cap covering a finger hole.

remember

marching band A group of musicians who play military (soldiers') music as they march along.

mellow A word used to describe a soft, warm, gentle sound.

mouth organ An instrument blown by the mouth that sounds like an organ.

mouthpiece The part of a wind or brass instrument held in the mouth, where it is blown.

musician Someone who plays an instrument or sings.

orchestra A large group of musicians playing together.

performer Someone who plays or sings to other people.

reed A tiny, thin piece of metal or cane that vibrates and makes the sound in some wind instruments.

rock A type of pop music, which often has a strong beat.

solo A piece of music played or sung by one performer.

valves Small buttons or levers that a brass instrument player presses in and out to make different notes.

vibrate To move up and down very quickly, like shaking. When air passes over a reed it vibrates.

wind band An orchestra of woodwind instruments.

Index